Air Fryer Desserts C

Easy & Delicious Best 100 Air Fryer Desserts Recipes ideas in 2021

Beck Wall

Table of Contents

Table of Contents

Cream Cheese Cookies

Prep time: 10 minutes

Cook time: 9 minutes

Servings: 12

INGREDIENTS

½ cup cream cheese, softened

¾ cup erythritol

1 tsp vanilla extract

1 egg

1 ½ cups almond flour

½ tsp salt

½ tsp baking powder

INSTRUCTIONS

Preheat your air fryer to 330 degrees F and prepare your air fryer tray with a piece of parchment.

Beat the cream cheese and erythritol together in a large bowl.

Add the eggs and vanilla and mix until the batter comes together.

Add the salt, baking powder, pumpkin spice seasoning and almond flour and mix until a nice, smooth batter forms.

Scoop the cookie dough onto the prepared sheet tray. You will want to leave about 2 inches between the cookie dough scoops as the dough will spread slightly. If needed, you can bake the cookies in batches.

Bake the cookies in the air fryer for 8-9 minutes or until golden brown on the edges.

Let cool on the sheet tray for 5 minutes before removing and enjoying!

Sweet Cauliflower Rice with Cherries

Prep time: 10 minutes

Cook time: 30 minutes

Servings: 4

INGREDIENTS

1 and ½ cups cauliflower rice

1 and ½ teaspoons cinnamon powder

1/3 cup stevia

2 tablespoons coconut butter, melted

2 apples, peeled, cored and sliced

1 cup natural apple juice

3 cups almond milk

½ cup cherries, dried

INSTRUCTIONS

In a pan that fits your air fryer, combine rice with cinnamon, stevia, butter, apples, apple juice, almond milk and cherries, toss, introduce in your air fryer and cook at 365 degrees F for 30 minutes.

Divide between bowls and serve.

Enjoy!

Bread Dough and Amaretto Dessert

Prep time: 10 minutes

Cook time: 12 minutes

Servings: 12

INGREDIENTS

1 pound bread dough

1 cup sugar

½ cup butter, melted

1 cup heavy cream

12 ounces chocolate chips

2 tablespoons amaretto liqueur

INSTRUCTIONS

Roll dough, cut into 20 slices and then cut each slice in halves.

Brush dough pieces with butter, sprinkle sugar, place them in your air fryer's basket after you've brushed it some butter, cook them at 350 degrees F for 5 minutes, flip them, cook for 3 minutes more and transfer to a platter.

Heat up a pan with the heavy cream over medium heat, add chocolate chips and stir until they melt.

Add liqueur, stir again, transfer to a bowl and serve bread dippers with this sauce.

Enjoy!

Lemon Shortbread

Prep time: 15 minutes

Cook time: 15 minutes

Servings: 8

INGREDIENTS

½ cup butter

½ cup swerve sweetener

1 tsp vanilla extract

1 cup almond flour

1 tsp salt

1 tsp lemon zest

INSTRUCTIONS

Preheat your air fryer to 300 degrees F and grease a 6 inch baking pan or tray.

Place the butter and swerve sweetener in a mixing bowl and beat until soft and fluffy.

Add the vanilla extract and lemon zest and beat again to incorporate fully.

Add the almond flour slowly, mixing it in a little at a time, until a smooth dough has formed.

Spread the shortbread batter in the prepared baking pan or tray and then place in the preheated air fryer.

Bake for 15 minutes or until the edges of the shortbread are golden brown.

Let cool for 10 minutes then flip the shortbread out of the pan, slice and enjoy while warm.

Cranberry Pudding

Prep time: 10 minutes

Cook time: 30 minutes

Servings: 4

INGREDIENTS

4 ounces dried cranberries, chopped

A drizzle of olive oil

4 ounces dried apricots, chopped

1 cup white flour

3 teaspoons baking powder

1 cup coconut sugar

1 teaspoon ginger powder

A pinch of cinnamon powder

15 tablespoons coconut butter

3 tablespoons maple syrup

3 tablespoons flax meal mixed with 3 tablespoons water

1 carrot, grated

INSTRUCTIONS

Grease a heatproof pudding pan with a drizzle of oil.

In a blender, mix flour with baking powder, sugar, cinnamon, ginger, butter, maple syrup and flax meal and pulse well.

Add dried fruits and carrot, fold them into the batter and spread this mix into the pudding mold.

Put the pudding in your air fryer and cook at 365 degrees F for 30 minutes.

Leave the pudding aside to cool down, slice and serve.

Enjoy!

Sour Cream-Blueberry Coffee Cake

Servings: 6

Cook time: 35 minutes

INGREDIENTS

1/2 cup butter, softened

1 cup white sugar

1 egg

1/2 cup sour cream

1/2 teaspoon vanilla extract

3/4 cup and 1 tablespoon all-purpose flour

1/2 teaspoon baking powder

1/8 teaspoon salt

1/2 cup fresh or frozen blueberries

1/4 cup brown sugar

1/2 teaspoon ground cinnamon

1/4 cup chopped pecans

1-1/2 teaspoons confectioners' sugar for dusting

INSTRUCTIONS

In a small bowl, whisk well pecans, cinnamon, and brown sugar.

In a blender, blend well all wet Ingredients. Add dry ingredients except for confectioner's sugar and blueberries. Blend well until smooth and creamy.

Lightly grease baking pan of air fryer with cooking spray.

Pour half of batter in pan. Sprinkle half of pecan mixture on top. Pour the remaining batter. And then topped with remaining pecan mixture.

Cover pan with foil.

For 35 minutes, cook on 330oF.

Serve and enjoy with a dusting of confectioner's sugar.

Pecan-Cranberry Cake

Servings: 6

Cook time: 25 minutes

INGREDIENTS

1/4 cup cashew milk (or use any dairy or non-dairy milk you prefer)

2 large eggs

1/2 tsp vanilla extract

1 1/2 cups Almond Flour

1/4 cup Monk fruit (or use your preferred sweetener)

1 tsp baking powder

1/4 tsp cinnamon

1/8 tsp salt

1/2 cup fresh cranberries

1/4 cup chopped pecans

INSTRUCTIONS

In blender, add all wet ingredients and mix well. Add all dry ingredients except for cranberries and pecans. Blend well until smooth.

Lightly grease baking pan of air fryer with cooking spray. Pour in batter. Drizzle cranberries on top and then followed by pecans.

For 20 minutes, cook on 330oF.

Let stand for 5 minutes.

Serve and enjoy.

Zucchini Bread

Prep time: 10 minutes

Cook time: 35 minutes

Servings: 6

INGREDIENTS

1 cup natural applesauce

1 ½ banana, mashed

1 tablespoon vanilla extract

4 tablespoons coconut sugar

2 cups zucchini, grated

2 and ½ cups coconut flour

½ cup baking cocoa powder

1 teaspoon baking soda

¼ teaspoon baking powder

1 teaspoon cinnamon powder

½ cup walnuts, chopped

Cooking spray

INSTRUCTIONS

Grease a loaf pan with cooking spray, add zucchini, sugar, vanilla, banana, applesauce, flour, cocoa powder, baking soda, baking powder, cinnamon and walnuts, whisk well, introduce in the fryer and cook at 365 degrees F for 35 minutes.

Leave the bread to cool down, slice and serve.

Enjoy!

Butter Cookies

Prep time: 10 minutes

Cook time: 9 minutes

Servings: 12

INGREDIENTS

½ cup butter, melted

¾ cup erythritol

1 tsp vanilla extract

1 egg

1 ½ cups almond flour

¼ tsp xanthan gum

½ tsp salt

½ tsp baking powder

INSTRUCTIONS

Preheat your air fryer to 330 degrees F and prepare your air fryer tray with a piece of parchment.

Beat the melted butter and erythritol together in a large bowl.

Add the eggs and vanilla and mix until the batter comes together.

Add the salt, baking powder, xanthan gum and almond flour and mix until a nice, smooth batter forms.

Scoop the cookie dough onto the prepared sheet tray. You will want to leave about 2 inches between the cookie dough scoops as the dough will spread slightly. If needed, you can bake the cookies in batches.

Bake the cookies in the air fryer for 8-9 minutes or until golden brown on the edges.

Let cool on the sheet tray for 5 minutes before removing and enjoying!

Crunchy Crisped Peaches

Servings: 4

Cook time: 30 minutes

INGREDIENTS

4cup sliced peaches, frozen

3tablespoon sugar

2tablespoon Flour, white

1teaspoon sugar, white

1/4 cup Flour, white

1/3 cup oats, dry rolled

3 tablespoon butter, unsalted

1 teaspoon cinnamon

3tablespoon pecans, chopped

INSTRUCTIONS

Lightly grease baking pan of air fryer with cooking spray. Mix in a tsp cinnamon, 2 tbsp flour, 3 tbsp sugar, and peaches.

For 20 minutes, cook on 300oF.

Mix the rest of the ingredients in a bowl. Pour over peaches.

Cook for 10 minutes at 330oF.

Serve and enjoy.

Peanut Butter Chocolate Cookies

Prep time: 10 minutes

Cook time: 9 minutes

Servings: 12

INGREDIENTS

¼ cup butter, melted

¼ cup peanut butter

¾ cup erythritol

1 tsp vanilla extract

1 egg

1 ¼ cups almond flour

¼ cup cocoa powder

½ tsp salt

½ tsp baking powder

INSTRUCTIONS

Preheat your air fryer to 330 degrees F and prepare your air fryer tray with a piece of parchment.

Beat the melted butter, peanut butter and erythritol together in a large bowl.

Add the eggs and vanilla and mix until the batter comes together.

Add the salt, baking powder, cocoa powder and almond flour and mix until a nice, smooth batter forms.

Scoop the cookie dough onto the prepared sheet tray. You will want to leave about 2 inches between the cookie dough scoops as the dough will spread slightly. If needed, you can bake the cookies in batches.

Bake the cookies in the air fryer for 8-9 minutes or until golden brown on the edges.

Let cool on the sheet tray for 5 minutes before removing and enjoying!

Cocoa Brownies

Prep time: 10 minutes

Cook time: 20 minutes

Servings: 12

INGREDIENTS

6 ounces coconut oil, melted

3 tablespoons flax meal combined with 3 tablespoons water

3 ounces cocoa powder

2 teaspoons vanilla

½ teaspoon baking powder

4 ounces coconut cream

5 tablespoons stevia

INSTRUCTIONS

In a blender, mix flax meal with oil, cocoa powder, baking powder, vanilla, cream and stevia and stir using a mixer.

Pour this into a lined baking dish that fits your air fryer, introduce in the fryer and cook at 350 degrees F for 20 minutes.

Slice into rectangles and serve cold

Enjoy!

Berries Salad

Prep time: 10 minutes

Cook time: 10 minutes

Servings: 4

INGREDIENTS

1 cup blackberries

1 cup blueberries

1 cup strawberries

1 cup mango, peeled and cubed

2 tablespoons sugar

1 cup coconut cream

INSTRUCTIONS

In the air fryer's pan, mix the berries with the other ingredients, toss and cook at 360 degrees F for 10 minutes.

Divide into bowls and serve cold.

Almond Shortbread

Prep time: 15 minutes

Cook time: 15 minutes

Servings: 8

INGREDIENTS

½ cup butter

½ cup swerve sweetener

1 tsp almond extract

1 cup almond flour

1 tsp salt

½ cup sliced almonds

INSTRUCTIONS

Preheat your air fryer to 300 degrees F and grease a 6 inch baking pan or tray.

Place the butter and swerve sweetener in a mixing bowl and beat until soft and fluffy.

Add the almond extract and beat again to incorporate fully.

Add the almond flour slowly, mixing it in a little at a time, until a smooth dough has formed.

Spread the shortbread batter in the prepared baking pan or tray and then sprinkle the sliced almonds over the top of the shortbread.

Place in the preheated air fryer and bake for 15 minutes or until the edges of the shortbread are golden brown.

Let cool for 10 minutes then flip the shortbread out of the pan, slice and enjoy while warm.

Chocolate Chip Shortbread

Prep time: 15 minutes

Cook time: 15 minutes

Servings: 8

INGREDIENTS

½ cup butter

½ cup swerve sweetener

1 tsp vanilla extract

1 cup almond flour

1 tsp salt

½ cup dark chocolate chips, unsweetened

INSTRUCTIONS

Preheat your air fryer to 300 degrees F and grease a 6 inch baking pan or tray.

Place the butter and swerve sweetener in a mixing bowl and beat until soft and fluffy.

Add the vanilla extract and beat again to incorporate fully.

Add the almond flour slowly, mixing it in a little at a time, until a smooth dough has formed.

Fold in the chocolate chips gently.

Spread the shortbread batter in the prepared baking pan or tray and then place in the preheated air fryer.

Bake for 15 minutes or until the edges of the shortbread are golden brown.

Let cool for 10 minutes then flip the shortbread out of the pan, slice and enjoy while warm.

Strawberry Pop Tarts

Servings: 6

Cook time: 25 minutes

INGREDIENTS

2 refrigerated pie crusts

1 tsp cornstarch

1/3 cup low-sugar strawberry preserves

1/2 cup plain, non-fat vanilla Greek yogurt

1 oz reduced-fat Philadelphia cream cheese

1 tsp sugar sprinkles

1 tsp stevia

olive oil or coconut oil spray

INSTRUCTIONS

Cut pie crusts into 6 equal rectangles.

In a bowl, mix cornstarch and preserves. Add preserves in middle of crust. Fold over crust. Crimp edges with fork to seal. Repeat process for remaining crusts.

Lightly grease baking pan of air fryer with cooking spray. Add pop tarts in single layer. Cook in batches for 8 minutes at 370oF.

Meanwhile, make the frosting by mixing stevia, cream cheese, and yogurt in a bowl. Spread on top of cooked pop tart and add sugar sprinkles.

Serve and enjoy.

Plums, Avocado and Grapes Stew

Prep time: 10 minutes

Cook time: 20 minutes

Servings: 4

INGREDIENTS

1 cup plums, pitted and halved

1 cup red grapes

1 cup avocado, peeled, pitted and cubed

2 tablespoons lime juice

1 cup water

2 tablespoons sugar

INSTRUCTIONS

In a pan that fits your air fryer, mix the plums with the grapes and the other ingredients, stir, introduce in the fryer and cook at 330 degrees F for 20 minutes.

Divide the mix into bowls and serve cold.

Ginger Cheesecake

Prep time: 2 hours and 10 minutes

Cook time: 20 minutes

Servings: 6

INGREDIENTS

2 teaspoons butter, melted

½ cup ginger cookies, crumbled

16 ounces cream cheese, soft

2 eggs

½ cup sugar

1 teaspoon rum

½ teaspoon vanilla extract

½ teaspoon nutmeg, ground

INSTRUCTIONS

Grease a pan with the butter and spread cookie crumbs on the bottom.

In a bowl, beat cream cheese with nutmeg, vanilla, rum and eggs, whisk well and spread over the cookie crumbs.

Introduce in your air fryer and cook at 340 degrees F for 20 minutes.

Leave cheesecake to cool down and keep in the fridge for 2 hours before slicing and serving it.

Enjoy!

Peanut Butter Chocolate Chip Cookies

Prep time: 10 minutes

Cook time: 9 minutes

Servings: 12

INGREDIENTS

¼ cup butter, melted

½ cup peanut butter

¾ cup erythritol

1 tsp vanilla extract

1 egg

1 ½ cups almond flour

½ tsp salt

½ tsp baking powder

¾ cup sugar free chocolate chips

INSTRUCTIONS

Preheat your air fryer to 330 degrees F and prepare your air fryer tray with a piece of parchment.

Beat the melted butter, peanut butter and erythritol together in a large bowl.

Add the eggs and vanilla and mix until the batter comes together.

Add the salt, baking powder and almond flour and mix until a nice, smooth batter forms.

Fold in the chocolate chips then scoop the cookie dough onto the prepared sheet tray. You will want to leave about 2 inches between the cookie dough scoops as the dough will spread slightly. If needed, you can bake the cookies in batches.

Bake the cookies in the air fryer for 8-9 minutes or until golden brown on the edges.

Let cool on the sheet tray for 5 minutes before removing and enjoying!

Banana Bread

Prep time: 10 minutes

Cook time: 40 minutes

Servings: 6

INGREDIENTS

¾ cup sugar

1/3 cup butter

1 teaspoon vanilla extract

1 egg

2 bananas, mashed

1 teaspoon baking powder

1 and ½ cups flour

½ teaspoons baking soda

1/3 cup milk

1 and ½ teaspoons cream of tartar

Cooking spray

INSTRUCTIONS

In a bowl, mix milk with cream of tartar, sugar, butter, egg, vanilla and bananas and stir everything.

In another bowl, mix flour with baking powder and baking soda.

Combine the 2 mixtures, stir well, pour this into a cake pan greased with some cooking spray, introduce in your air fryer and cook at 320 degrees F for 40 minutes.

Take bread out, leave aside to cool down, slice and serve it.

Enjoy!

Air Fryed Churros with Choco Dip

Servings: 12

Cook time: 30 minutes

INGREDIENTS

1/2 cup water

1/4 teaspoon kosher salt

1/4 cup , plus 2 Tbsp. unsalted butter, divided

1/2 cup (about 2 1/8 oz.) all-purpose flour

2 large eggs

1/3 cup granulated sugar

2 teaspoons ground cinnamon

4 ounces bittersweet baking chocolate, finely chopped

3 tablespoons heavy cream

2 tablespoons vanilla kefir

INSTRUCTIONS

In small saucepan, bring to a boil ¼ cup butter, salt, and water. Stir in flour and lower fire to a simmer. Cook until smooth and thickened and pulls away from side of pan.

Transfer dough to a bowl and stir constantly until cooled.

Stir in eggs one at a time.

Transfer to a pastry bag with a star tip. Chill for half an hour.

Lightly grease baking pan of air fryer with cooking spray. Pipe dough on bottom of pan in 3-inch lengths.

For 10 minutes, cook on 3900F. Halfway through Cook time, shake. Cook in batches

In a small bowl mix cinnamon and sugar. In another bowl, place melted butter.

Brush cooked churros with melted butter and then roll in sugar mixture.

In microwave safe bowl, melt cream and chocolate. Mix well and stir in vanilla.

10)Serve and enjoy with dip on the side.

Pumpkin Spice Cookies

Prep time: 10 minutes

Cook time: 9 minutes

Servings: 12

INGREDIENTS

¼ cup butter, melted

¼ cup pumpkin puree

¾ cup erythritol

1 tsp vanilla extract

1 egg

1 ½ cups almond flour

½ tsp salt

1 tsp pumpkin spice seasoning

½ tsp baking powder

INSTRUCTIONS

Preheat your air fryer to 330 degrees F and prepare your air fryer tray with a piece of parchment.

Beat the melted butter, pumpkin puree and erythritol together in a large bowl.

Add the eggs and vanilla and mix until the batter comes together.

Add the salt, baking powder, pumpkin spice seasoning and almond flour and mix until a nice, smooth batter forms.

Scoop the cookie dough onto the prepared sheet tray. You will want to leave about 2 inches between the cookie dough scoops as the dough will spread slightly. If needed, you can bake the cookies in batches.

Bake the cookies in the air fryer for 8-9 minutes or until golden brown on the edges.

Let cool on the sheet tray for 5 minutes before removing and enjoying!

Figs and Grapes Bowls

Prep time: 10 minutes

Cook time: 15 minutes

Servings: 4

INGREDIENTS

2 cups red grapes

2 tablespoons sugar

1 cup heavy cream

2 cups figs, halved

½ teaspoon nutmeg powder

INSTRUCTIONS

In your air fryer's pan, combine the figs with the grapes and the other ingredients, toss and cook at 360 degrees F for 15 minutes.

Divide into bowls and serve.

Espresso Vanilla Dessert

Prep time: 10 minutes

Cook time: 20 minutes

Servings: 4

INGREDIENTS

1 cup almond milk

4 tablespoons flax meal

2 tablespoons coconut flour

2 and ½ cups water

2 tablespoons stevia

1 teaspoon espresso powder

2 teaspoons vanilla extract

Coconut cream for serving

INSTRUCTIONS

In a pan that fits your air fryer, mix flax meal with flour, water, stevia, milk, vanilla and espresso powder, stir, introduce in the fryer and cook at 365 degrees F for 20 minutes.

Divide into bowls and serve with coconut cream on top.

Enjoy!

Air Fryed Peach Pies

Servings: 8

Cook time: 24 minutes

INGREDIENTS

2 (5-oz.) fresh peaches, peeled and chopped

1 tablespoon fresh lemon juice (from 1 lemon)

3 tablespoons granulated sugar

1 teaspoon vanilla extract

1/4 teaspoon table salt

1 teaspoon cornstarch

1 (14.1-oz.) pkg. refrigerated piecrusts

INSTRUCTIONS

In medium bowl, whisk well salt, vanilla, sugar, and lemon juice. Let stand for 15 minutes while stirring every now and then. Drain while reserving a tablespoon of the liquid.

In reserved liquid mix in cornstarch and then stir into drained peaches.

Slice crusts into 8 pieces of 4-inch circles. Add a tablespoon of peach filling. Brush sides of dough with water, fold in half and crimp edge with fork to seal dough. Repeat to remaining doughs.

Lightly grease air fryer basket with cooking spray. Add dough in a single layer and cook in batches.

For 8 minutes, cook on 3900F.

Serve and enjoy.

Lemon Blueberry Cake

Servings: 4

Cook time: 17 minutes

INGREDIENTS

2 1/2 cups self-rising flour

1/2 cup Monk Fruit (or use your preferred sugar)

1/2 cup cream

1/4 cup avocado oil (any light cooking oil)

2 eggs

1 cup blueberries

zest from 1 lemon

juice from 1 lemon

1 tsp. vanilla

brown sugar for topping (a little sprinkling on top of each muffin-less than a teaspoon)

INSTRUCTIONS

In mixing bowl, beat well wet Ingredients. Stir in dry ingredients and mix thoroughly.

Lightly grease baking pan of air fryer with cooking spray. Pour in batter.

For 12 minutes, cook on 330oF.

Let it stand in air fryer for 5 minutes.

Serve and enjoy.

Caramel Dip 'n Apple Fries

Servings: 8

Cook time: 16 minutes

INGREDIENTS

3 Pink Lady or Honeycrisp apples, peeled, cored and cut into 8 wedges

½ cup flour

3 eggs, beaten

1 cup graham cracker crumbs

¼ cup sugar

8 ounces whipped cream cheese

½ cup caramel sauce, plus more for garnish

INSTRUCTIONS

In a large bowl, toss well flour and apple slices.

In one bowl beat eggs. In another bowl mix well, sugar and graham crackers.

Dredge apple slices in egg and then roll in graham mixture.

Lightly grease air fryer basket with cooking spray. Add a single layer of apples. Cook in batches for 8 minutes at 390oF.

Meanwhile, mix caramel sauce and whipped cream cheese..

Serve and enjoy with the dip on the side.

Enchanting Coffee-Apple Cake

Servings: 6

Cook time: 40 minutes

INGREDIENTS

2 tablespoons butter, softened

1/4 cup and 2 tablespoons brown sugar

1/2 large egg

2 tablespoons sour cream

2 tablespoons vanilla yogurt

1/2 teaspoon vanilla extract

1/2 cup all-purpose flour

1/4 teaspoon ground cinnamon

1/4 teaspoon baking soda

1/8 teaspoon salt

1 cup diced Granny Smith apple

Topping ingredients

2 tablespoons brown sugar

2 tablespoons all-purpose flour

1 tablespoon butter

1/4 teaspoon ground cinnamon

INSTRUCTIONS

In blender, puree all wet Ingredients. Add dry ingredients except for apples and blend until smooth. Stir in apples.

Lightly grease baking pan of air fryer with cooking spray. Pour batter into pan.

In a small bowl mix well, all topping ingredients and spread on top of cake batter.

Cover pan with foil.

For 20 minutes, cook on 3300F.

Remove foil and cook for 10 minutes. Let it stand in air fryer for another 10 minutes.

Serve and enjoy.

Tasty Banana Cake

Prep time: 10 minutes

Cook time: 30 minutes

Servings: 4

INGREDIENTS

1 tablespoon butter, soft

1 egg

1/3 cup brown sugar

2 tablespoons honey

1 banana, peeled and mashed

1 cup white flour

1 teaspoon baking powder

½ teaspoon cinnamon powder

Cooking spray

INSTRUCTIONS

Spray a cake pan with some cooking spray and leave aside.

In a bowl, mix butter with sugar, banana, honey, egg, cinnamon, baking powder and flour and whisk

Pour this into a cake pan greased with cooking spray, introduce in your air fryer and cook at 350 degrees F for 30 minutes.

Leave cake to cool down, slice and serve.

Enjoy!

Out-of-this-World PB&J Doughnuts

Servings: 6

Cook time: 30 minutes

INGREDIENTS

1 1/4 Cups all-purpose flour

1/3 Cup sugar

1/2 Teaspoon baking powder

1/2 Teaspoon baking soda

3/4 Teaspoon salt

1 Egg

1/2 Cup buttermilk

1 Teaspoon vanilla

2 Tablespoons unsalted butter, melted and cooled

1 Tablespoon melted butter for brushing the tops

Filling Ingredient:

1/2 Cup Blueberry or strawberry jelly (not preserves)

Glaze Ingredients

1/2 Cup powdered sugar

2 Tablespoons milk

2 Tablespoons peanut butter

Pinch of sea salt

INSTRUCTIONS

In mixing bowl, whisk well all wet Ingredients. Mix in dry ingredients and beat until thoroughly combined. Roll dough to ¾-inch thickness. Cut into 3.5-inch rounds.

Lightly grease baking pan of air fryer with cooking spray. Add doughnuts in single layer. Cook in batches at for 10 minutes at 3300F.

Meanwhile, make the glaze by mixing all ingredients in a bowl.

Fill each doughnut with filling and spread glaze on top.

Serve and enjoy.

Butter and bread pudding

Prep time: 10-20 minutes

Cook time: 15-30 minutes

Servings: 4

INGREDIENTS

5/6 slices of honey bread

30 g butter

20 g raisins

400 ml of milk

4 egg yolks

90 g of sugar

Cinnamon to taste

1 vanilla pod

DIRECTION:

Remove the crust from the slices of bread and spread the butter on each slice, place them in the container previously buttered.

Pour the raisins over the bread. Separately, beat the eggs and sugar with an electric mixer and then add the milk (previously heated with the vanilla pod) until a very homogeneous mixture is obtained.

Pour the mixture over the slices of bread, being careful to distribute it evenly. Sprinkle with sugar and cinnamon.

Cook at 160oC for 30 minutes or until desired browning is achieved.

Serve hot with whipped cream or jam.

Thai Fish Cake with Mango Sauce

Prep time: 20 minutes

Cook time: 14 minutes

Servings: 4

INGREDIENTS

1 ripe mango

1 tsp and a half of red chili paste

3 tbsp fresh cilantro or parsley

1 lime juice and zest

500 g of white fish fillets

1 egg

1 chopped chive

50 g ground coconut

DIRECTION:

Peel the mango and cut it into small dice. Mix the mango dice in a bowl with ½ teaspoon of red chili paste, 1 tablespoon of cilantro and the juice and zest of a lime.

Beat the fish in the kitchen robot and mix it with 1 egg, 1 teaspoon of salt and the rest of the lime zest, red chili paste and lime juice. Mix everything with the rest of the cilantro, chives and 2 tablespoons of coconut.

Place the rest of the coconut on a deep plate. Divide the fish mixture into 12 portions, shape them in round cakes and coat them with the coconut.

Place six fish cakes in the basket and place it in the air fryer at 180°C. Set the timer to 7 minutes and fry the cakes until golden brown and ready to drink. Fry in the same way the rest of the fish cakes.

Serve with mango sauce.

Easy Buns

Prep time: 10 minutes

Cook time: 30 minutes

Servings: 8

INGREDIENTS

½ cup coconut flour

1/3 cup psyllium husks

2 tablespoons stevia

1 teaspoon baking powder

½ teaspoon cinnamon powder

½ teaspoon cloves, ground

3 tablespoons flax meal combined with 3 tablespoons water

Some chocolate chips, unsweetened

INSTRUCTIONS

In a bowl, mix flour with psyllium husks, swerve, baking powder, salt, cinnamon, cloves and chocolate chips and stir well.

Add water and flax meal, stir well until you obtain a dough, shape 8 buns and arrange them on a lined baking sheet.

Introduce in the air fryer and cook at 350 degrees for 30 minutes.

Serve these buns warm.

Fresh Pizza

Prep time: 10-20 minutes

Cook time: 30-45 minutes

Servings: 1

INGREDIENTS

70ml of water

125 g flour

3g salt

7 g fresh yeast

100 g of tomato

100 g mozzarella

Oregano to taste

DIRECTION:

Pour the flour into a bowl, form a well, and then add the other ingredients in the center.

Knead with your hands until you get soft and flexible dough. Form a ball with this dough, and then let it grow in a previously floured bowl.

Cover with a clean cloth and let stand at room temperature, away from drafts. After about 1 hour of lifting, start spreading the dough

Preheat the air fryer to 1500C for 5 minutes.

Grease the bottom and spread the pizza dough. Cover with tomato coulis. Add a pinch of salt and oregano.

After 15 minutes cook add the diced mozzarella

Approximately after 10 minutes, turn the pizza half a turn

Cook for an additional 7 minutes.

Easy-Peasy Apple Pie

Servings: 4

Cook time: 35 minutes

INGREDIENTS

1 Pillsbury Refrigerator pie crust

Baking spray

1 large apple, chopped

2 teaspoons lemon juice

1 tablespoon ground cinnamon

2 tablespoon sugar

½ teaspoon vanilla extract

1 tablespoon butter

1 beaten egg

1 tablespoon raw sugar

INSTRUCTIONS

Lightly grease baking pan of air fryer with cooking spray. Spread pie crust on bottom of pan up to the sides.

In a bowl, mix vanilla, sugar, cinnamon, lemon juice, and apples. Pour on top of pie crust. Top apples with butter slices.

Cover apples with the other pie crust. Pierce with knife the tops of pie.

Spread beaten egg on top of crust and sprinkle sugar.

Cover with foil.

For 25 minutes, cook on 390oF.

Remove foil cook for 10 minutes at 330oF until tops are browned.

Serve and enjoy.

bread pudding

Prep time: 10-20 minutes

Cook time: 15-30 minutes

Servings: 4

INGREDIENTS

5/6 slices of honey bread

30 g butter

20 g raisins

400 ml of milk

4 egg yolks

90 g of sugar

Cinnamon to taste

1 vanilla pod

DIRECTION:

Remove the crust from the slices of bread and spread the butter on each slice, place them in the container previously buttered.

Pour the raisins over the bread. Separately, beat the eggs and sugar with an electric mixer and then add the milk (previously heated with the vanilla pod) until a very homogeneous mixture is obtained.

Pour the mixture over the slices of bread, being careful to distribute it evenly. Sprinkle with sugar and cinnamon.

Cook at 1600C for 30 minutes or until desired browning is achieved.

Serve hot with whipped cream or jam.

Risotto with Porcini Mushrooms

Prep time: 0-10 minutes

Cook time: 15-30 minutes

Servings: 6

INGREDIENTS

320 g of basmati rice

200 g of porcini mushrooms

1250ml of broth

1 clove garlic

Parsley to taste

Grated cheese to taste

Butter to taste

DIRECTION:

Grease the basket and add the garlic clove.

Set the temperature to 150oC and brown for 2 minutes.

Remove the garlic, add the porcini mushrooms and simmer for another 5 minutes.

Add the rice, half the amount of the broth and simmer for another 10 minutes.

Pour the rest of the broth and finish cooking for another 13 minutes. Mix 2-3 times with a ladle at the end of cooking.

At the end of cooking, add the chopped parsley and mix with butter and grated cheese, serve.

Cream and Pine Nuts Cake

Prep time: more than 30 minutes

Cook time: 45-60 minutes

Servings: 10

INGREDIENTS

250 g flour

125 g butter

110 g of sugar

2 eggs (1 whole and egg yolk)

Salt to taste

500ml pastry cream

120 g of pine nuts

DIRECTION:

Remove the flour, sugar, eggs, butter nuts from the refrigerator and a pinch of salt in the blender.

Mix everything until you get a compact and quite flexible mixture. Let it rest in the refrigerator for at least 30 minutes.

Butter and flour the basket. Spread the mass of broken dough with a thickness of ¾ cm and place it at the bottom of the basket, carefully cutting the edge.

Prick with a fork and spread the custard with a spoon.

Finish the cake by covering it completely with pine nuts.

Set the air fryer to 180oC.

Cook for 40 minutes and then turn off the lower resistance.

Cook another 15 minutes. Cool the cake well before turning it over to turn it off.

Ricotta Cake

Prep time: 10 minutes

Cook time: 40 minutes

Servings: 10

INGREDIENTS

250 g flour

200 g of sugar

Eggs

350 g ricotta

120 g melted butter

1 sachet of yeast

50 g of chocolate chips

DIRECTION:

Add ricotta with sugar, add eggs and melted butter. Add the sifted flour with the yeast and finally the chocolate chips.

Butter and flour the basket and pour the mixture inside, smearing well.

Set the temperature to 1800C and bake the cake for 40 minutes.

Let cool and remove it from the basket; sprinkle with icing sugar.

Ricotta Cake and Chocolate Chips

Prep time: 10-20 minutes

Cook time: 45-60 minutes

Servings: 10

INGREDIENTS

For the dough:

380g flour

165 g of sugar

185 g of butter

2 eggs

1 egg yolk

1 pinch of salt

Ingredients for filling:

600 g ricotta

1 lemon zest

100 g of chocolate chips

DIRECTION:

Put the flour, sugar, eggs, butter in pieces just outside the refrigerator and a pinch of salt in a blender. Mix everything until you get a compact and sufficiently elastic mixture. Let it rest in the fridge for at least half an hour.

Grease and flour the basket. Unroll the mass of broken dough to a thickness of 3-4 mm and cover the bottom and walls. In a bowl, beat the ricotta with the eggs, the sugar, and the lemon zest until you get a smooth and smooth mixture. Finally, add the chocolate chips.

Pour everything inside the baking sheet covered with broken dough and slightly bend the edges inwards.

Set the temperature to 1800C.

Cook for 40 minutes and then turn off the lowest resistance. Cook for another 10 minutes. Cool well before removing from the baking sheet.

Mushroom, Egg and Mozzarella Cake

Prep time: 10 minutes

Cook time: 50 minutes

Servings: 6

INGREDIENTS

2 rolls of puff pastry: 2

300 g mushrooms

1 onion

Parsley to taste

150 g mozzarella

3 eggs

DIRECTION:

Clean the mushrooms well and chop them.

Spray the basket of the air fryer. Pour the chopped onion in the basket

Brown for 2 minutes at 1600C.

Add the mushrooms and cook for another 15 minutes. Add (at discretion) salt and pepper, parsley, and finish cooking for another 3 minutes. Meanwhile, prepare hard boiled eggs.

In a bowl, mix the mushrooms with the crushed eggs and the chopped mozzarella, salt, and pepper.

Unroll the broken dough (leaving the baking paper) and then prick the bottom with a fork.

Arrange the egg and mushroom mixture and close with the other dough roll. Weld the edges well.

Brush the surface of the dough with egg yolk and prick the steam out.

Bake the cake for 30 minutes.

Roasted pears

Prep time: 5 minutes

Cook time: 20 minutes

Servings: 2

INGREDIENTS

4 portions

4 pears with rind well washed

50 g Raisins

2 tbsp jam without sugar

1 tsp honey

1 pinch cinnamon powder

DIRECTION:

Pears are washed, hollowed out by extracting the heart.

Separate the pulp

Mix the jam chosen with the pulp of pears, honey and raisins and cinnamon

Fill the pears with that mixture

Place the pears in the fryer

In the bowl place a glass of water

Cook for 20 minutes at 1800C

Serve them alone or accompanied with a scoop of vanilla ice cream.

Chia Pudding

Prep time: 10 minutes

Cook time: 20 minutes

Servings: 4

INGREDIENTS

½ cup tapioca pearls, rinsed

1 and ½ cups almond milk

3 tablespoons sugar

½ teaspoon vanilla extract

½ teaspoon nutmeg, ground

INSTRUCTIONS

In your air fryer's pan, mix the tapioca with the almond milk and the other ingredients, whisk, put the pan in the fryer and cook at 340 degrees F for 20 minutes.

Divide the pudding into bowls and serve.

Rice and Grapes Pudding

Prep time: 5 minutes

Cook time: 20 minutes

Servings: 4

INGREDIENTS

1 cup white rice

2 cups almond milk

½ cup grapes, halved

3 tablespoons sugar

1 teaspoon ginger, ground

1 tablespoon heavy cream

1 teaspoon vanilla extract

INSTRUCTIONS

In a pan that fits your air fryer, mix the rice with the milk and the other ingredients, whisk, introduce the pan in the fryer and cook at 360 degrees F for 20 minutes.

Divide the mix into bowls and serve cold.

Maple Chia Bowls

Prep time: 10 minutes

Cook time: 20 minutes

Servings: 4

INGREDIENTS

4 tablespoons chia seeds

1 tablespoon maple syrup

1 cup almond milk

½ cup raisins

2 tablespoons sugar

1 teaspoon vanilla extract

INSTRUCTIONS

In a pan that fits your air fryer, mix the chia seeds with the maple syrup and the other ingredients, toss, introduce in the fryer and cook at 360 degrees F for 20 minutes.

Divide into bowls and serve cold.

Orange and Raisins Bowls

Prep time: 10 minutes

Cook time: 20 minutes

Servings: 4

INGREDIENTS

½ pound oranges, peeled and cut into segments

1 cup raisins

1 cup heavy cream

2 tablespoons honey

½ teaspoon vanilla extract

INSTRUCTIONS

In a pan that fits your air fryer, mix the oranges with the raisins and the other ingredients, put the pan in the fryer and cook at 340 degrees F for 20 minutes.

Divide into bowls and serve cold.

Apricot Jam

Prep time: 10 minutes

Cook time: 25 minutes

Servings: 6

INGREDIENTS

1 pound apricots, chopped

1 cup sugar

1 teaspoon almond extract

Juice of 1 lime

2 cups water

INSTRUCTIONS

In a pan that fits your air fryer, mix the apricots with the sugar and the other ingredients, stir, introduce the pan in the fryer and cook at 360 degrees F for 25 minutes.

Blend the mix using an immersion blender, divide into bowls and serve cold.

Berries and Plums Jam

Prep time: 10 minutes

Cook time: 20 minutes

Servings: 6

INGREDIENTS

1 cup plums, pitted and chopped

1 cup blackberries

½ cup sugar

2 cups water

1 teaspoon almond extract

INSTRUCTIONS

In a pan that fits your air fryer, mix the plums with the berries and the other ingredients, stir, introduce in the fryer and cook at 360 degrees F for 20 minutes.

Divide into bowls and serve cold.

Grapes Cream

Prep time: 10 minutes

Cook time: 20 minutes

Servings: 4

INGREDIENTS

1 cup green grapes

1 cup heavy cream

3 tablespoons sugar

1 teaspoon almond extract

1 teaspoon cinnamon powder

INSTRUCTIONS

In a pan that fits your air fryer, mix the grapes with the cream and the other ingredients, introduce in the fryer, cook at 330 degrees F for 20 minutes, blend using an immersion blender, divide into bowls and serve.

Pears and Avocado Bowls

Prep time: 10 minutes

Cook time: 20 minutes

Servings: 4

INGREDIENTS

4 pears, cored and cut into wedges

1 cup avocado, peeled, pitted and cubed

1 cup apple juice

2 tablespoons sugar

½ teaspoon vanilla extract

INSTRUCTIONS

In the air fryer's cake pan, combine the pears with the avocado and the other ingredients, toss, put the pan in the fryer, and cook at 350 degrees F for 20 minutes.

Divide into bowls and serve.

Simple White Cake

Prep time: 10 minutes

Cook time: 30 minutes

Servings: 6

INGREDIENTS

1 cup white flour

½ cup white chocolate, melted

½ cup heavy cream

1 teaspoon almond extract

2 eggs, whisked

1 teaspoon baking soda

4 tablespoons sugar

2 tablespoons butter, melted

Cooking spray

INSTRUCTIONS

In a bowl, mix the chocolate with the flour and the other ingredients except the cooking spray and stir well.

Grease the air fryer's cake pan with the cooking spray, pour the cake mix and spread into the pan.

Put the pan in the fryer, cook at 360 degrees F for 30 minutes, cool down, slice and serve.

Spiced Cream

Prep time: 10 minutes

Cook time: 20 minutes

Servings: 4

INGREDIENTS

1 cup heavy cream

1 cup coconut cream

2 tablespoons sugar

1 teaspoon nutmeg, ground

1 teaspoon cinnamon powder

1 teaspoon ginger, ground

INSTRUCTIONS

In a bowl, mix the cream with the sugar and the other ingredients, whisk well and divide into 4 ramekins.

Put the ramekins in the air fryer, cook at 350 degrees F for 20 minutes, cool down and serve.

Nutmeg Apples Bowls

Prep time: 10 minutes

Cook time: 20 minutes

Servings: 4

INGREDIENTS

1 pound green apples, cored and cut into wedges

1 teaspoon nutmeg, ground

2 tablespoons brown sugar

½ cup apple juice

INSTRUCTIONS

In your air fryer's pan, combine the apples with the nutmeg and the other ingredients, and cook at 350 degrees F for 20 minutes.

Divide the mix into bowls and serve.

Pumpkin and Apples Bowls

Prep time: 10 minutes

Cook time: 20 minutes

Servings: 4

INGREDIENTS

2 cups pumpkin flesh, chopped

2 cups apples, cored and cubed

1 cup heavy cream

3 tablespoons sugar

1 teaspoon vanilla extract

1 teaspoon nutmeg, ground

1 teaspoon cinnamon powder

INSTRUCTIONS

In the air fryer's pan, mix the pumpkin with the apples and the other ingredients, toss, put the pan in the machine, cook at 360 degrees F for 20 minutes, cool down, divide into bowls and serve.

Grapes, Apples and Mango Salad

Prep time: 10 minutes

Cook time: 15 minutes

Servings: 4

INGREDIENTS

1 cup green grapes

1 cup apples, cored and cubed

1 cup mango, peeled and cubed

1 cup heavy cream

½ teaspoon cinnamon powder

2 tablespoons sugar

INSTRUCTIONS

In your air fryer's pan, mix the grapes with the apples and the other ingredients, toss and cook at 320 degrees F for 15 minutes.

Divide the mix into bowls and serve.

Pears Bowls

Prep time: 5 minutes

Cook time: 20 minutes

Servings: 4

INGREDIENTS

1 pound pears, cored and cut into wedges

1 cup apple juice

½ cup pineapple, peeled and cubed

2 tablespoon sugar

INSTRUCTIONS

In your air fryer's pan, combine the pears with the apple juice and the other ingredients, toss and cook at 330 degrees F for 20 minutes.

Divide the mix into bowls and serve.

Chocolate Cherries Mix

Prep time: 10 minutes

Cook time: 20 minutes

Servings: 4

INGREDIENTS

2 cups cherries, pitted and halved

1 cup dark chocolate, melted

1 cup coconut cream

2 tablespoons cocoa powder

1 tablespoon sugar

½ teaspoon lemon juice

INSTRUCTIONS

In the air fryer's pan, combine the cherries with the chocolate and the other ingredients, introduce the pan in the fryer and cook at 360 degrees F for 20 minutes.

Divide into bowls and serve.

Banana and Grapes Bowls

Prep time: 10 minutes

Cook time: 20 minutes

Servings: 4

INGREDIENTS

2 cups bananas, peeled and sliced

2 cups red grapes

1 cup heavy cream

3 tablespoons sugar

Juice of 1 lime

INSTRUCTIONS

In the air fryer's pan, combine the bananas with the grapes and the other ingredients, toss, put it in your machine and cook at 330 degrees F for 20 minutes.

Divide into bowls and serve.

Grapes Cake

Prep time: 10 minutes

Cook time: 30 minutes

Servings: 6

INGREDIENTS

1 cup grapes, chopped

3 tablespoons sugar

1 cup almond flour

1 cup heavy cream

1 teaspoon vanilla extract

2 eggs, whisked

1 tablespoon baking powder

3 tablespoons butter, melted

Cooking spray

INSTRUCTIONS

In a bowl, mix the grapes with the sugar and the other ingredients except the cooking spray and stir well.

Grease the air fryer's pan with the cooking spray, pour the cake mix inside, and cook at 350 degrees F for 30 minutes.

Cool down, slice and serve.

Creamy Almond and Rice

Prep time: 10 minutes

Cook time: 25 minutes

Servings: 4

INGREDIENTS

1 cup white rice

2 cups almond milk

½ cup almonds, chopped

3 tablespoons sugar

1 teaspoon vanilla extract

1/3 cup heavy cream

INSTRUCTIONS

In your air fryer's pan, combine the rice with the milk and the other ingredients and cook at 350 degrees F for 25 minutes

Divide the mix into bowls and serve.

Orange, Grapes and Rhubarb Mix

Prep time: 10 minutes

Cook time: 20 minutes

Servings: 4

INGREDIENTS

2 tablespoons sugar

1 cup oranges, peeled and cut into segments

1 cup rhubarb, sliced

1 cup red grapes

1 cup milk

2 tablespoons orange juice

INSTRUCTIONS

In the air fryer's pan, mix the oranges with the rhubarb and the other ingredients, toss and cook at 320 degrees F for 20 minutes.

Divide into bowls and serve cold.

Mango Cake

Prep time: 10 minutes

Cook time: 35 minutes

Servings: 8

INGREDIENTS

1 and ½ cups mango, peeled and chopped

1 and ½ cups almond flour

¾ teaspoon baking powder

3 eggs, whisked

1 cup heavy cream

3 tablespoons sugar

¼ cup coconut milk

4 tablespoons butter, melted

Cooking spray

INSTRUCTIONS

In a bowl, mix the mango with the flour, eggs and the other ingredients except the cooking spray and whisk well.

Pour this into a cake pan that fits your air fryer greased with cooking spray, transfer to your air fryer, cook at 360 degrees F for 35 minutes, cool down, cut and serve.

Vanilla Strawberry Mix

Prep time: 10 minutes

Cook time: 20 minutes

Servings: 10

INGREDIENTS

2 tablespoons lemon juice

2 pounds strawberries

4 cups coconut sugar

1 teaspoon cinnamon powder

1 teaspoon vanilla extract

INSTRUCTIONS

In a pan that fits your air fryer, mix strawberries with coconut sugar, lemon juice, cinnamon and vanilla, stir gently, introduce in the fryer and cook at 350 degrees F for 20 minutes

Divide into bowls and serve cold.

Enjoy!

Sweet Bananas and Sauce

Prep time: 10 minutes

Cook time: 20 minutes

Servings: 4

INGREDIENTS

Juice of ½ lemon

3 tablespoons agave nectar

1 tablespoon coconut oil

4 bananas, peeled and sliced diagonally

½ teaspoon cardamom seeds

INSTRUCTIONS

Arrange bananas in a pan that fits your air fryer, add agave nectar, lemon juice, oil and cardamom, introduce in the fryer and cook at 360 degrees F for 20 minutes

Divide bananas and sauce between plates and serve.

Enjoy!

Orange Cake with Raisins

Prep time: 10 minutes

Cook time: 30 minutes

Servings: 4

INGREDIENTS

Cooking spray

1 teaspoon baking powder

1 cup almond flour

1 cup coconut sugar

½ teaspoon cinnamon powder

3 tablespoons coconut oil, melted

½ cup almond milk

½ cup pecans, chopped

¾ cup water

½ cup raisins

½ cup orange peel, grated

¾ cup orange juice

INSTRUCTIONS

In a bowl, mix flour with half of the sugar, baking powder, cinnamon, 2 tablespoons oil, milk, pecans and raisins, stir and pour this in a greased cake pan that fits your air fryer.

Heat up a small pan over medium heat, add water, orange juice, orange peel, the rest of the oil and the rest of the sugar, stir, bring to a boil, pour over the mix from the pan, introduce in the fryer and cook at 330 degrees F for 30 minutes.

Serve cold.

Enjoy!

Stuffed Apples

Prep time: 10 minutes

Cook time: 25 minutes

Servings: 5

INGREDIENTS

5 apples, tops cut off and cored

5 figs

1/3 cup coconut sugar

¼ cup pecans, chopped

2 teaspoons lemon zest, grated

½ teaspoon cinnamon powder

1 tablespoon lemon juice

1tablespoon coconut oil

INSTRUCTIONS

In a bowl mix figs, coconut sugar, pecans, lemon zest, cinnamon, lemon juice and coconut oil and stir.

Stuff the apples with this mix, introduce them in your air fryer and cook at 365 degrees F for 25 minutes.

Enjoy!

Cinnamon Apples and Mandarin Sauce

Prep time: 10 minutes

Cook time: 20 minutes

Servings: 4

INGREDIENTS

4 apples, cored, peeled and cored

2 cups mandarin juice

¼ cup maple syrup

2 teaspoons cinnamon powder

1 tablespoon ginger, grated

INSTRUCTIONS

In a pan that fits your air fryer, mix apples with mandarin juice, maple syrup, cinnamon and ginger, introduce in the fryer and cook at 365 degrees F for 20 minutes

Divide apples mix between plates and serve warm.

Enjoy!

Almond Cookies

Prep time: 10 minutes

Cook time: 30 minutes

Servings: 12

INGREDIENTS

1 tablespoon flaxseed mixed with 2 tablespoons water

¼ cup coconut oil, melted

1 cup coconut sugar

½ teaspoon vanilla extract

1 teaspoon baking powder

1 and ½ cups almond meal

½ cup almonds, chopped

INSTRUCTIONS

In a bowl, mix oil with sugar, vanilla extract and flax meal and whisk.

Add baking powder, almond meal and almonds and stir well.

Spread cookie mix on a lined baking sheet, introduce in your air fryer and cook at 340 degrees F for 30 minutes.

Leave cookie sheet to cool down, cut into medium pieces and serve.

Enjoy!

Ginger Pumpkin Cake

Prep time: 10 minutes

Cook time: 40 minutes

Servings: 10

INGREDIENTS

1 and ½ teaspoons baking powder

Cooking spray

1 cup pumpkin puree

2 cups almond flour

½ teaspoon baking soda

1 and ½ teaspoons cinnamon, ground

¼ teaspoon ginger, ground

1 tablespoon coconut oil, melted

1 tablespoon flaxseed mixed with 2 tablespoons water

1 tablespoon vanilla extract

1/3 cup maple syrup

1 teaspoon lemon juice

INSTRUCTIONS

In a bowl, flour with baking powder, baking soda, cinnamon and ginger and stir.

Add flaxseed, coconut oil, vanilla, pumpkin puree, maple syrup and lemon juice, stir and pour into a greased cake pan.

Introduce in your air fryer, cook at 330 degrees F for 40 minutes, leave aside to cool down, slice and serve.

Enjoy!

Sweet Potato Mix

Prep time: 10 minutes

Cook time: 30 minutes

Servings: 8

INGREDIENTS

1 cup water

1 tablespoon lemon peel, grated

½ cup coconut sugar

3 sweet potatoes peeled and sliced

¼ cup cashew butter

¼ cup maple syrup

1 cup pecans, chopped

INSTRUCTIONS

In a pan that fits your air fryer, mix water with lemon peel, coconut sugar, potatoes, cashew butter, maple syrup and pecans, stir, introduce in the fryer and cook at 350 degrees F for 30 minutes

Divide sweet potato pudding into bowls and serve cold.

Enjoy!

Cinnamon Rice with Coconut

Prep time: 10 minutes

Cook time: 35 minutes

Servings: 4

INGREDIENTS

3 and ½ cups water

1 cup coconut sugar

2 cups white rice, washed and rinsed

2 cinnamon sticks

½ cup coconut, shredded

INSTRUCTIONS

In your air fryer, mix water with coconut sugar, rice, cinnamon and coconut, stir, cover and cook at 365 degrees F for 35 minutes.

Divide pudding into cups and serve cold.

Enjoy!

Chocolate Vanilla Bars

Prep time: 10 minutes

Cook time: 7 minutes

Servings: 12

INGREDIENTS

1 cup sugar free and vegan chocolate chips

2 tablespoons coconut butter

2/3 cup coconut cream

2 tablespoons stevia

¼ teaspoon vanilla extract

INSTRUCTIONS

Put the cream in a bowl, add stevia, butter and chocolate chips and stir

Leave aside for 5 minutes, stir well and mix the vanilla.

Transfer the mix into a lined baking sheet, introduce in your air fryer and cook at 356 degrees F for 7 minutes.

Leave the mix aside to cool down, slice and serve.

Enjoy!

Raspberry Bars

Prep time: 10 minutes

Cook time: 6 minutes

Servings: 12

INGREDIENTS

½ cup coconut butter, melted

½ cup coconut oil

½ cup raspberries, dried

¼ cup swerve

½ cup coconut, shredded

INSTRUCTIONS

In your food processor, blend dried berries very well.

In a bowl that fits your air fryer, mix oil with butter, swerve, coconut and raspberries, toss well, introduce in the fryer and cook at 320 degrees F for 6 minutes.

Spread this on a lined baking sheet, keep in the fridge for an hour, slice and serve.

Enjoy!

Blueberry Squares

Prep time: 10 minutes

Cook time: 20 minutes

Servings: 8

INGREDIENTS

5 ounces coconut oil, melted

½ teaspoon baking powder

4 tablespoons stevia

1 teaspoon vanilla

4 ounces coconut cream

3 tablespoons flax meal combined with 3 tablespoons water

½ cup blueberries

INSTRUCTIONS

In a bowl, mix coconut oil with flax meal, coconut cream, vanilla, stevia and baking powder and blend using an immersion blender.

Fold blueberries, pour everything into a square baking dish that fits your air fryer, introduce in the fryer and cook at 320 degrees F for 20 minutes.

Slice into squares and serve cold.

Enjoy!

Blackberries Coconut Scones

Prep time: 10 minutes

Cook time: 10 minutes

Servings: 10

INGREDIENTS

½ cup coconut flour

1 cup blackberries

2 tablespoons flax meal combined with 2 tablespoons water

½ cup coconut cream

½ cup coconut butter

½ cup almond flour

5 tablespoons stevia

2 teaspoons vanilla extract

2 teaspoons baking powder

INSTRUCTIONS

In a bowl, mix almond flour with coconut flour, baking powder and blackberries and stir well.

In another bowl, mix cream with butter, vanilla extract, stevia and flax meal and stir well.

Combine the 2 mixtures, stir until you obtain your dough, shape 10 triangles from this mix, place them on a lined baking sheet, introduce in the air fryer and cook at 350 degrees F for 10 minutes.

Serve them cold.

Enjoy!

Lemon and Banana Cream

Prep time: 10 minutes

Cook time: 30 minutes

Servings: 6

INGREDIENTS

1 and 1/3 pint almond milk

1 medium banana

4 tablespoons lemon zest, grated

3 tablespoons flax meal combined with 3 tablespoons water

5 tablespoons stevia

2 tablespoons lemon juice

INSTRUCTIONS

In a bowl, mix mashed banana with milk and swerve and stir very well.

Add lemon zest and lemon juice, whisk well, pour into ramekins, place them in your air fryer, cook at 360 degrees F for 30 minutes and serve cold.

Enjoy!

Cocoa Berries Cream

Prep time: 10 minutes

Cook time: 10 minutes

Servings: 4

INGREDIENTS

3 tablespoons cocoa powder

14 ounces coconut cream

1 cup blackberries

1 cup raspberries

2 tablespoons stevia

INSTRUCTIONS

In a bowl, whisk cocoa powder with stevia and cream and stir.

Add raspberries and blackberries, toss gently, transfer to a pan that fits your air fryer, introduce in the fryer and cook at 350 degrees F for 10 minutes.

Divide into bowls and serve cold.

Enjoy!

Cocoa Pudding

Prep time: 10 minutes

Cook time: 20 minutes

Servings: 2

INGREDIENTS

2 tablespoons water

½ tablespoon agar

4 tablespoons stevia

4 tablespoons cocoa powder

2 cups coconut milk, hot

INSTRUCTIONS

In a bowl, mix milk with stevia and cocoa powder and stir well.

In a bowl, mix agar with water, stir well, add to the cocoa mix, stir and transfer to a pudding pan that fits your air fryer.

Introduce in the fryer and cook at 356 degrees F for 20 minutes.

Serve the pudding cold.

Enjoy!

Blueberry Coconut Crackers

Prep time: 10 minutes

Cook time: 30 minutes

Servings: 12

INGREDIENTS

½ cup coconut butter

½ cup coconut oil, melted

1 cup blueberries

3 tablespoons coconut sugar

INSTRUCTIONS

In a pan that fits your air fryer, mix coconut butter with coconut oil, raspberries and sugar, toss, introduce in the fryer and cook at 367 degrees F for 30 minutes

Spread on a lined baking sheet, keep in the fridge for a few hours, slice crackers and serve.

Enjoy!

Cauliflower Pudding

Prep time: 10 minutes

Cook time: 30 minutes

Servings: 4

INGREDIENTS

2 and ½ cups water

1 cup coconut sugar

2 cups cauliflower rice

2 cinnamon sticks

½ cup coconut, shredded

INSTRUCTIONS

In a pan that fits your air fryer, mix water with coconut sugar, cauliflower rice, cinnamon and coconut, stir, introduce in the fryer and cook at 365 degrees F for 30 minutes

Divide pudding into cups and serve cold.

Enjoy!

Sweet Vanilla Rhubarb

Prep time: 10 minutes

Cook time: 10 minutes

Servings: 4

INGREDIENTS

5 cups rhubarb, chopped

2 tablespoons coconut butter, melted

1/3 cup water

1 tablespoon stevia

1 teaspoon vanilla extract

INSTRUCTIONS

Put rhubarb, ghee, water, stevia and vanilla extract in a pan that fits your air fryer, introduce in the fryer and cook at 365 degrees F for 10 minutes

Divide into small bowls and serve cold.

Enjoy!

Pineapple and Apricots

Prep time: 10 minutes

Cook time: 12 minutes

Servings: 10

INGREDIENTS

6 cups canned pineapple chunks, drained

4 cups canned apricots, halved and drained

3 cups natural applesauce

2 cups canned mandarin oranges, drained

2 tablespoons stevia

1 teaspoon cinnamon powder

INSTRUCTIONS

Put pineapples, apricots, applesauce, oranges, cinnamon and stevia in a pan that fits your air fryer, introduce in the fryer and cook at 360 degrees F for 12 minutes.

Divide into small bowls and serve cold.

Enjoy!

Brownie with Salty Pistachio

Servings: 4

Cook time: 25 minutes

INGREDIENTS

1/4 cup nondairy milk

1/4 cup aquafaba

1/2 teaspoon vanilla extract

1/2 cup whole wheat pastry flour

1/2 cup vegan sugar

1/4 cup cocoa powder

1 tablespoon ground flax seeds

1/4 teaspoon salt

INSTRUCTIONS

In a large bowl, whisk well all dry Ingredients. Beat in the wet ingredients until combined thoroughly.

Lightly grease baking pan of air fryer with cooking spray. Pour in batter and evenly spread.

For 20 minutes, cook on preheated 330oF air fryer.

Let it sit for 5 minutes.

Serve and enjoy.

Garlic Knots with Parmesan

Servings: 12

Cook time: 16 minutes

INGREDIENTS

1 13.8 oz refrigerated pizza crust

3 tbsp Olive oil

3 tbsp Minced garlic

Garlic salt

Parmesan cheese powder

INSTRUCTIONS

Roll dough out onto a cutting board. Cut dough into equal ¼" strips. Wrap each strip into knots

Mix olive oil & garlic in a bowl. Dip each knot into the mixture.

Lightly grease baking pan of air fryer with cooking spray. Add knots in a single layer and cook in batches for 4 minutes at 390oF.

Dust with Parmesan.

Serve and enjoy.

Creamy Leche Flan

Servings: 4

Cook time: 30 minutes

INGREDIENTS

1/3 cup white sugar

1/2 (14 ounce) can sweetened condensed milk

1 cup heavy cream

1/2 cup milk

2-1/2 eggs

1 teaspoon vanilla extract

INSTRUCTIONS

In blender, blend well vanilla, eggs, milk, cream, and condensed milk.

Lightly grease baking pan of air fryer with cooking spray. Add sugar and heat for 10 minutes at 370oF until melted and caramelized. Lower heat to 300oF and continue melting and swirling.

Pour milk mixture into caramelized sugar. Cover pan with foil.

Cook for 20 minutes at 330oF.

Let it cool completely in the fridge.

Place a plate on top of pan and invert pan to easily remove flan.

Serve and enjoy.

Sugared Doughs with Choco Dip

Servings: 10

Cook time: 24 minutes

INGREDIENTS

1-pound bread dough, defrosted

½ cup butter, melted

¾ to 1 cup sugar

1 cup heavy cream

12 ounces good quality semi-sweet chocolate chips

2 tablespoons Amaretto liqueur (or almond extract)

INSTRUCTIONS

Roll the dough into two 15-inch logs. Cut each log into 20 slices. Cut each slice in half and twist the dough halves together 3 to 4 times. Place the twisted dough on a cookie sheet, brush with melted butter and sprinkle sugar over the dough twists.

Lightly grease air fryer basket with cooking spray. Add dough twists in a single layer. Cook in batches for 8 minutes at 390oF. Halfway through Cook time, shake basket and brush with butter. Once done cooking dip in a bowl of sugar.

Meanwhile make the dip by heating cream in microwave. Stir in chocolate and heat again until melted and thoroughly combined. Stir in amaretto. And set aside for dipping.

Serve and enjoy.

Blackberry-Goodness Cobbler

Servings: 5

Cook time: 20 minutes

INGREDIENTS

1/4 cup white sugar

1 tablespoon cornstarch

3 cups fresh blackberries

2 tablespoons melted butter

1-1/4 cups all-purpose flour

3/4 cup white sugar

1-1/2 teaspoons baking powder

1/2 teaspoon salt

1 cup milk

1-1/2 teaspoons vanilla extract

2 tablespoons melted butter

INSTRUCTIONS

Lightly grease baking pan of air fryer with cooking spray. Add blackberries and drizzle with 2 tbsps. melted butter.

In a small bowl, whisk cornstarch and 1/4 cup sugar. Sprinkle over blackberries and toss well to coat.

In another bowl, whisk well salt, baking powder, and ¾ cup sugar. Stir in 2 tbsps. melted butter, vanilla, and milk. Mix well and pour over berries.

For 20 minutes, cook on 390oF or until tops are lightly browned.

Serve and enjoy.

Easy 'n Delicious Brownies

Servings: 8

Cook time: 20 minutes

INGREDIENTS

1/4 cup butter

1/2 cup white sugar

1 egg

1/2 teaspoon vanilla extract

2 tablespoons and 2 teaspoons unsweetened cocoa powder

1/4 cup all-purpose flour

1/8 teaspoon salt

1/8 teaspoon baking powder

Frosting ingredients

1 tablespoon and 1-1/2 teaspoons butter, softened

1 tablespoon and 1-1/2 teaspoons unsweetened cocoa powder

1-1/2 teaspoons honey

1/2 teaspoon vanilla extract

1/2 cup confectioners' sugar

INSTRUCTIONS

Lightly grease baking pan of air fryer with cooking spray. Melt ¼ cup butter for 3 minutes. Stir in vanilla, eggs, and sugar. Mix well.

Stir in baking powder, salt, flour, and cocoa mix well. Evenly spread.

For 20 minutes, cook on 3000F.

In a small bowl, make the frosting by mixing well all Ingredients. Frost brownies while still warm.

Serve and enjoy.

Simple Cheesecake

Prep time: 10 minutes

Cook time: 15 minutes

Servings: 15

INGREDIENTS

1 pound cream cheese

½ teaspoon vanilla extract

2 eggs

4 tablespoons sugar

1 cup graham crackers, crumbled

2 tablespoons butter

INSTRUCTIONS

In a bowl, mix crackers with butter.

Press crackers mix on the bottom of a lined cake pan, introduce in your air fryer and cook at 350 degrees F for 4 minutes.

Meanwhile, in a bowl, mix sugar with cream cheese, eggs and vanilla and whisk well.

Spread filling over crackers crust and cook your cheesecake in your air fryer at 310 degrees F for 15 minutes.

Leave cake in the fridge for 3 hours, slice and serve.

Enjoy!

Bread Pudding

Prep time: 10 minutes

Cook time: 1 hour

Servings: 4

INGREDIENTS

6 glazed doughnuts, crumbled

1 cup cherries

4 egg yolks

1 and ½ cups whipping cream

½ cup raisins

¼ cup sugar

½ cup chocolate chips.

INSTRUCTIONS

In a bowl, mix cherries with egg yolks and whipping cream and stir well.

In another bowl, mix raisins with sugar, chocolate chips and doughnuts and stir.

Combine the 2 mixtures, transfer everything to a greased pan that fits your air fryer and cook at 310 degrees F for 1 hour.

Chill pudding before cutting and serving it.

Enjoy!

Amandine Pistachio Cake

Prep time: more than 30 minutes

Cook time: 30 – 45 minutes

Servings: 8

INGREDIENTS

For the broken dough:

250 g flour

110 g of sugar

125 g butter

2 eggs

Salt to taste

DIRECTION:

Broken dough:

Remove flour, sugar, eggs, butter nuts from the refrigerator and a pinch of salt in the blender.

Mix everything until you get a compact and quite flexible mixture. Let it rest in the refrigerator for at least 30 minutes.

Almond cream:

Put the chopped almonds, sugar in a blender, and mix everything, then add the flour, eggs and mix well. Separately, cut the pistachios and cut them into large pieces.

Butter and flour the bottom of the basket. Unroll the broken dough leaving an edge that may contain almond cream. Prick with a fork and spread the jam.

Spread the almond cream and distribute the chopped pine nuts and pistachios.

Cook for 45 minutes at 1800C

Let cool and sprinkle with icing sugar.

Carrot Cake

Prep time: 10 minutes

Cook time: 45 minutes

Servings: 6

INGREDIENTS

5 ounces flour

¾ teaspoon baking powder

½ teaspoon baking soda

½ teaspoon cinnamon powder

¼ teaspoon nutmeg, ground

½ teaspoon allspice

1 egg

3 tablespoons yogurt

½ cup sugar

¼ cup pineapple juice

4 tablespoons sunflower oil

1/3 cup carrots, grated

1/3 cup pecans, toasted and chopped

1/3 cup coconut flakes, shredded

Cooking spray

INSTRUCTIONS

1. In a bowl, mix flour with baking soda and powder, salt, allspice, cinnamon and nutmeg and stir.
2. In another bowl, mix egg with yogurt, sugar, pineapple juice, oil, carrots, pecans and coconut flakes and stir well.
3. Combine the two mixtures and stir well, pour this into a spring form pan that fits your air fryer which you've greased with some cooking spray, transfer to your air fryer and cook on 320 degrees F for 45 minutes.
4. Leave cake to cool down, then cut and serve it.
5. Enjoy!

Speck and Cheese Roll

Prep time: 10 – 20 minutes

Cook time: 0 – 15 minutes

Servings: 6

INGREDIENTS

1 roll of puff pastry

6 speck slices

4 slices of provola (spun cheese)

DIRECTION:

Unroll the puff pastry and spread the speck slices.

Place the cheese slices on the speck and roll the puff pastry until you get a roll. Weld well.

Cut the roll into slices and place it inside the mold lined with baking paper.

Set the temperature to 180oC.

Cook the rolls for 13 minutes or according to the desired degree of cooking.

Potatoes with Small Bacon

Prep time: 10-20 minutes

Cook time: 30-45 minutes

Servings: 8

INGREDIENTS

1250 g of fresh potatoes(peeled)

100 g smoked bacon

Salt and pepper to taste

1 sprig rosemary

DIRECTION:

Peel the potatoes and cut them into quarters. Put the potatoes in the water for a few minutes and rinse them well. Drain and clean with a paper towel.

Pour the potatoes, rosemary in the basket previously greased, season with salt and pepper.

Set the temperature to 1500C and cook for 15 minutes.

Add the bacon and finish cooking, simmer for another 20 minutes.

Double Chocolate Cookies

Prep time: 10 minutes

Cook time: 9 minutes

Servings: 12

INGREDIENTS

½ cup butter, melted

¾ cup erythritol

1 tsp vanilla extract

1 egg

1 ¼ cups almond flour

¼ cup cocoa powder

½ tsp salt

½ tsp baking powder

¾ cup unsweetened chocolate chips

INSTRUCTIONS

Preheat your air fryer to 330 degrees F and prepare your air fryer tray with a piece of parchment.

Beat the melted butter and erythritol together in a large bowl.

Add the eggs and vanilla and mix until the batter comes together.

Add the salt, baking powder, cocoa powder and almond flour and mix until a nice, smooth batter forms.

Fold in the chocolate chips then scoop the cookie dough onto the prepared sheet tray. You will want to leave about 2 inches between the cookie dough scoops as the dough will spread slightly. If needed, you can bake the cookies in batches.

Bake the cookies in the air fryer for 8-9 minutes or until golden brown on the edges.

Let cool on the sheet tray for 5 minutes before removing and enjoying!

Amazing with Every Bite Fried Bananas

Servings: 4

Cook time: 12 minutes

INGREDIENTS

4 Ripe Bananas, peeled and sliced in half crosswise and then in half lengthwise

2 tablespoons All Purpose Flour (Maida)

2 tablespoons Rice flour

2 tablespoons Corn flour

2 tablespoons Desiccated Coconut Powder

1 pinch Salt

1/2 teaspoon Baking powder

INSTRUCTIONS

Make the batter by mixing coconut, salt, baking powder, corn flour, rice flour, and Maida in a bowl. Add bananas and cover well in mixture.

Lightly grease air fryer basket with cooking spray. Add bananas.

For 12 minutes, cook on 3900F. Halfway through Cook time, shake basket.

Serve and enjoy.

Baked Potatoes

Prep time: 0-10 minutes

Cook time: more than 60 minutes

Servings: 4

INGREDIENTS

4 whole potatoes (230 g each)

4 slices of cheddar cheese

20 g butter

4 slices of bacon

Salt to taste

Pepper to taste

DIRECTION:

Wash potatoes well, brushing them gently to remove all traces of dirt without damaging the skin.

Cover each potato with oil and cover with a handful of salt (this will make the skin crisp).

Place the potatoes in the basket of the pan on parchment paper.

Set the air fryer to 1600C. Simmer for 60 min. (the time varies according to the size of the potatoes used), therefore, it will be useful to verify from time to time that the cooking is perfect.

After cooking, cut the potatoes crosswise and dig a little inside. Cover each potato with a piece of butter, a slice of bacon and a slice of cheese.

Sprinkle with black pepper and always brown with the thermostat in position 4 for another 3 minutes.

Apple-Blueberry Crumble Vegan Approved

Servings: 2

Cook time: 15 minutes

INGREDIENTS

1 medium apple, finely diced

½ cup frozen blueberries, strawberries, or peaches

¼ cup plus 1 tablespoon brown rice flour

2 tablespoons sugar

½ teaspoon ground cinnamon

2 tablespoons nondairy butter

INSTRUCTIONS

Lightly grease baking pan of air fryer with cooking spray.

Spread frozen blueberries and apple slices on bottom of pan.

In a bowl, whisk well butter, cinnamon, sugar, and flour. Sprinkle over fruit. If needed, sprinkle extra flour to cover exposed fruit.

For 15 minutes, cook on 3300F

Serve and enjoy.

Gluten-Free Yogurt Cake

Prep time: 10 minutes

Cook time: 40 minutes

Servings: 2

INGREDIENTS

1 Greek yogurt

3 eggs

150 g sugar

100 g cream

50 g sunflower oil

50 g butter

200 g gluten free flour

Salt

1 on yeast

DIRECTION:

Put the eggs, yogurt, and sugar in the basket. Mix well. Add the rest of the ingredients and mix.

Put the dough in the sponge cake container, previously brushed with oil. Preheat the fryer and put the mold with the dough for 40 minutes at 170°C.

When it cools, unmold, and decorate to taste.

Mini Lava Cakes

Prep time: 10 minutes

Cook time: 20 minutes

Servings: 3

INGREDIENTS

1 egg

4 tablespoons sugar

2 tablespoons olive oil

4 tablespoons milk

4 tablespoons flour

1 tablespoon cocoa powder

½ teaspoon baking powder

½ teaspoon orange zest

INSTRUCTIONS

In a bowl, mix egg with sugar, oil, milk, flour, salt, cocoa powder, baking powder and orange zest, stir very well and pour this into greased ramekins.

Add ramekins to your air fryer and cook at 320 degrees F for 20 minutes.

Serve lava cakes warm.

Enjoy!

Cocoa Cake

Prep time: 10 minutes

Cook time: 17 minutes

Servings: 6

INGREDIENTS

35 ounces butter, melted

3 eggs

3 ounces sugar

1 teaspoon cocoa powder

3 ounces flour

½ teaspoon lemon juice

INSTRUCTIONS

In a bowl, mix 1 tablespoon butter with cocoa powder and whisk.

In another bowl, mix the rest of the butter with sugar, eggs, flour and lemon juice, whisk well and pour half into a cake pan that fits your air fryer.

Add half of the cocoa mix, spread, add the rest of the butter layer and top with the rest of cocoa.

Introduce in your air fryer and cook at 360 degrees F for 17 minutes.

Cool cake down before slicing and serving.

Enjoy!

Made in the USA
Columbia, SC
20 December 2023

29157152R00059